KNIGHTS AND CASTLES

Castle Life

Laura Durman

W

FRANKLIN WATTS
LONDON • SYDNEY

First published in 2012 by Franklin Watts

Franklin Watts
338 Euston Road
London
NW1 3BH

Franklin Watts Australia
Level 17/207 Kent Street, Sydney, NSW 2000

Produced by Arcturus Publishing Limited,
26/27 Bickels Yard, 151-153 Bermondsey Street, London SE1 3HA

Series Concept: Discovery Books Ltd.
www.discoverybooks.net
Editor for Discovery Books: Laura Durman
Designer: Ian Winton

Picture credits: Château des Baux de Provence http://chateau-baux-provence.com: pp 7, 11 (Culturespaces 2007), 24 (Culturespaces/A. Penillard); Corbis: pp 17 (Robert Holmes); Getty Images: pp 15 (Stock Montage / Contributor), 16 (The Bridgeman Art Library / French School); John James: p 26; Kris Katchit: p 22t; Shutterstock Images: cover (Kachalkina Veronika / Jim Lopes), title page and p 4 (aguilarphoto), pp 8 (Gail Johnson), 12 (Richardzz), 13t (Boykov), 13b (Bobby Deal / RealDealPhoto), 14 (Conde), 18 (Isa Ismail), 20b (FXQuadro), 22b (Pedro Talens Masip), 27 (Sergey Kamshylin), 28 (Stanislaw Tokarski); Peter Dennis: pp 6, 9, 10, 20t, 25; Mike White: p 21; Wikimedia Commons: pp 19, 23, 29.

A CIP catalogue record for this book is available from the British Library.

Dewey Decimal Classification Number: 940.1-dc23

ISBN: 978 1 4451 0998 5

Franklin Watts is a division of Hachette Children's Books, an Hachette UK company.
www.hachette.co.uk

Printed in China

SL002131EN
Supplier 03, Date 0412, Print run 1455

Contents

You might imagine that living in a medieval castle would be luxurious and romantic. It often looks that way in books and films. However, in reality, castle life was not always easy.

The **Middle Ages**, or the **medieval** period, was a time of wars and violence. Many castles were built from the 10th to 15th centuries to provide protection.

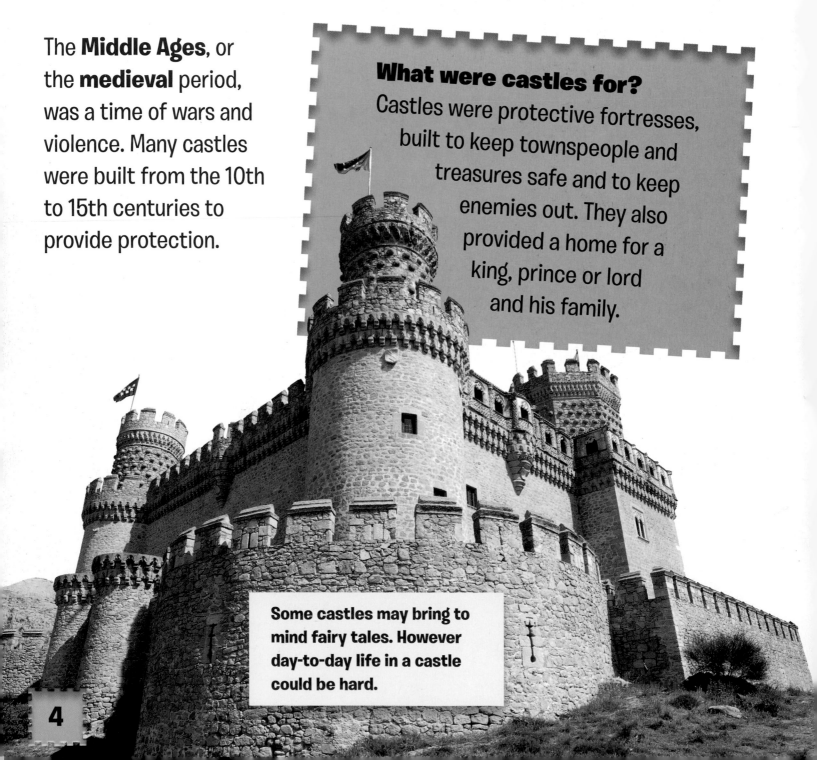

What were castles for?
Castles were protective fortresses, built to keep townspeople and treasures safe and to keep enemies out. They also provided a home for a king, prince or lord and his family.

Some castles may bring to mind fairy tales. However day-to-day life in a castle could be hard.

Castles were full of activity and noise. The largest castles had many servants who dashed from job to job, their days full of hard work. The sounds of **livestock**, orders being shouted, weapons being made and, occasionally, musicians filled the air.

Despite the hustle and bustle, castles were cold and dark places. They had no central heating or electric lighting. Large fireplaces warmed some parts of the castle, but they were mostly draughty and damp.

ALTERNATIVE HEATING

As well as the few fires, the body heat of people inside the castle helped to make it warmer.

This lord is lucky enough to have a warm fire in his bedroom.

Castle society

Castle life was strictly governed by the medieval feudal system. The system was like a pyramid with the king at the top. Under the king were nobles. Knights served the nobles and peasants served everyone above them.

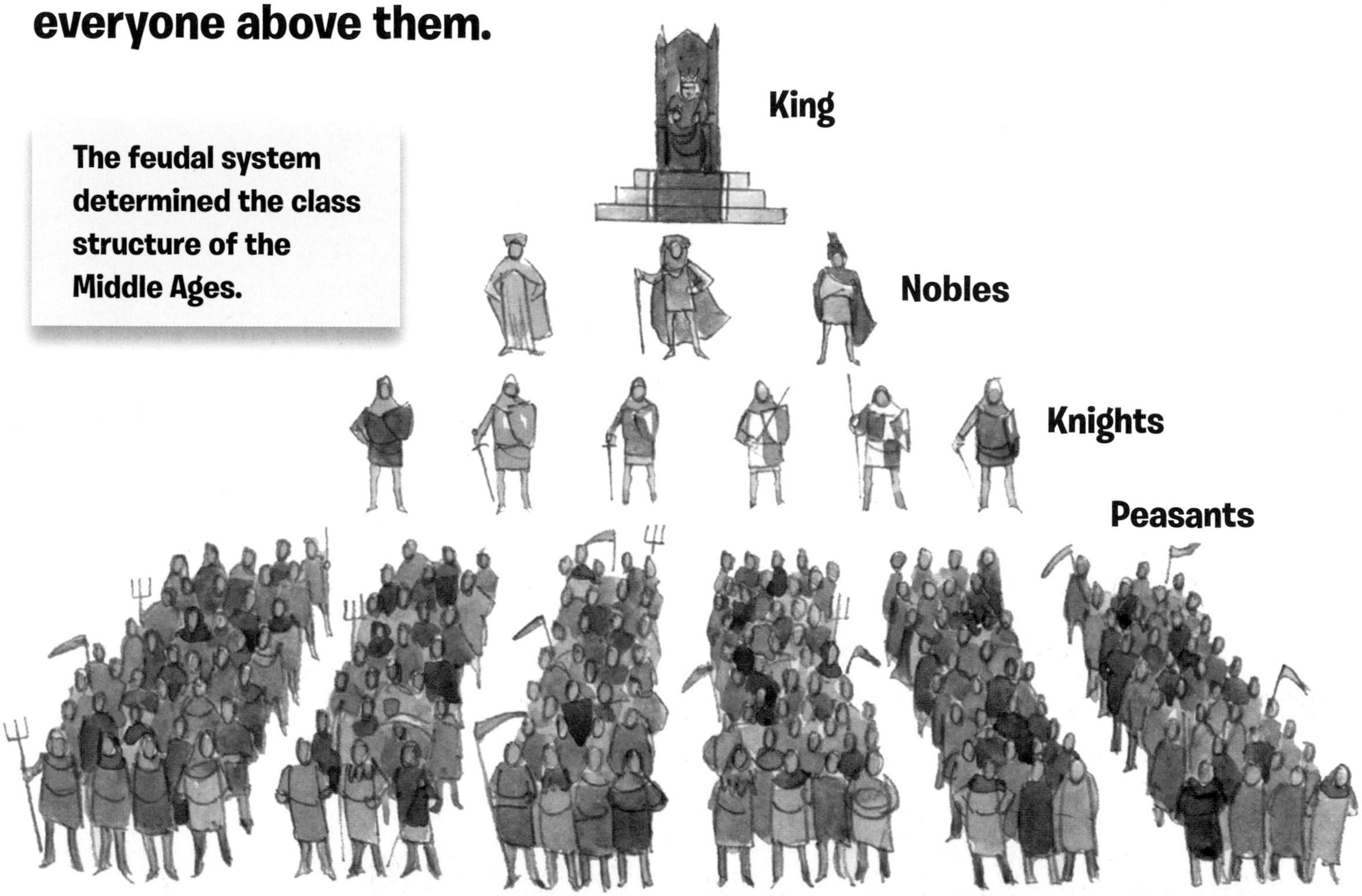

The feudal system determined the class structure of the Middle Ages.

King

Nobles

Knights

Peasants

During the Middle Ages, the king was the most powerful person in the country. However, he needed the support of important and wealthy nobles, such as lords, who would fight for him during a war. So the king gave portions of land to the nobles and gave them permission to build castles on the land.

Knights were soldiers bound to protect the lord and his family. During the early Middle Ages, knights often lived in the lord's castle. However, knights eventually became wealthy men and were able to buy their own land.

In this modern re-enactment, peasants celebrate the arrival of knights who will protect the castle during a **siege**.

At the bottom of the pyramid was the peasant class. Peasants lived and worked on the lord's land in exchange for protection. However, peasants had very few rights. They were forced to hand over a large share of the **produce** that they grew to the lords. This often left them struggling to survive.

You cannot wear that!

Clothing was also affected by the feudal system. Laws dictated what people in the different classes were allowed to wear. Rich castle owners wore clothing made from expensive fabrics, such as silk, velvet, satin and furs. In contrast, peasants wore clothes made of linen and wool.

The great hall was used by everyone who lived in the castle and was the heart of castle life. Privacy was limited, with only the castle owner and his family having rooms for personal use.

The great hall

This was the main meeting and dining room in a castle and contained large banqueting tables and a fireplace. The great hall was often painted, with **tapestries** hanging from the walls. The trampled earth floor may have been covered with straw and, depending on the owner's wealth, scented with herbs.

The great hall was the setting for castle feasts and banquets. There were often long banqueting tables, such as this one, with a separate table at one end for the lord and his family.

The kitchen

This was another very important room in the castle. Kitchens contained huge ovens and fires for smoking and roasting food. They also linked with other rooms such as the pantry, where food was prepared; the buttery, where drink was stored; and the scullery, where dishes were washed.

The solar

This was a suite of rooms used by the lord's family. The solar often contained a private sitting room and a wardrobe. The wardrobe was a dressing room in which clothes and treasures were stored.

This illustration shows the bedroom of a wealthy lady. She enjoys a bath in front of a roaring fire, while maids attend to her and make her bed.

Bedrooms

The sleeping chambers used by the lord and his relatives contained wooden beds with feather mattresses and quilts. These rooms were usually heated by a fire. However, the servants and workers slept on the floor of the great hall using their cloaks as covers.

Domestic jobs

The workers in a castle were expected to make the life of the lord and his companions as comfortable as possible. There were many different types of job to do within the castle household.

Constable

The constable was the most important employee. As communication was difficult in medieval times, lords often spent their time travelling. They left their castles in the capable hands of a constable.

Steward

The steward was in charge of all the domestic staff in the castle. He also made sure that there was enough food stored to feed the castle's **inhabitants** for up to a year.

The castle kitchens bustled with workers, including the chief cook, the **butler** and the **pantler**.

Tasters

Food tasters and cupbearers had the unfortunate job of sampling food and drink before it was served to the lord. They checked that the food was neither past its best nor poisoned. Although the job was risky, it was also well paid.

Castle security

The watchmen and men-at-arms were responsible for the security of the castle. They were assisted by young lookouts.

Castles needed guarding at all times. Men-at-arms and watchmen lived in the castle and were ready to defend it when necessary. They were under the constable's command.

Garderobe cleaner

The gong scourer, or gong farmer, probably had the worst job of all. It was his responsibility to clean and unblock the garderobes (medieval toilets).

NICOLA DE LA HAYE

It was relatively unusual for a woman to hold the post of constable in a castle. However, during the 12th century, Nicola de la Haye became constable of Lincoln Castle. She famously defended the castle during a siege in 1217.

Castle trades

As well as the domestic staff, many other workers lived within the castle walls. They included craftsmen and labourers, as well as skilled workers who provided services to the lord and his employees.

The bailiff was in charge of all the tradespeople who lived and worked in the castle. He **allotted** jobs to peasants and ensured that the castle and its weapons were kept in good repair. The reeve worked alongside the bailiff. He made sure that the workers began and stopped work on time, and that they did not steal from the castle.

Blacksmiths were kept very busy **forging** and sharpening weapons and tools. Armourers made metal armour that fitted each soldier. Armourers combined the metal-working skills of a blacksmith with the skills of a tailor.

Blacksmiths were very important castle workers. Not only did they shoe the horses and forge weapons, they also repaired all of the other workmen's tools.

HIGHLY-SKILLED AND HIGHLY-PAID

The attiliator made crossbows for the soldiers to use in battle. Attiliators were the most skilled craftsmen in the castle and were often paid 50 percent more than the others.

Animals were important to castle life and needed to be cared for. For example, grooms looked after the castle's horses. Falconers cared for and trained hawks for the popular sport of **falconry**.

Falconry was extremely popular in the Middle Ages. Skilled falconers were employed at every castle to train hawks for the sport.

Let there be light

Candles were an important source of light in the dark rooms of a castle. So the chandler, or candle-maker, was kept extremely busy. In the 11th century Graham Overhill, a chandler, created a candle-clock. The candle had 12 lines on it and it took an hour to burn to each one.

This modern re-enactment shows how candles were made in medieval times.

Castle life was very structured, with tasks and rituals performed at specific times throughout the day.

Guards blew their trumpets to wake the castle residents at sunrise. Servants rushed to light the fires and began preparing the day's main meal in the kitchens. Once the lord and lady had risen, a small breakfast was eaten in the great hall.

The castle trumpeters were the equivalent of a modern-day alarm clock. They blew their trumpets at sunrise to wake the castle household.

Sunrise start

As there were no electric lights in medieval times, the castle household rose at dawn to make the most of the daylight.

After breakfast, the lord and lady went to the chapel for **Mass** and to pray. The lord then dealt with business matters, such as hearing reports of the crops harvested and taxes collected on his land.

The main meal of the day was served at mid-morning and often had several courses. Musicians called minstrels sometimes entertained the diners during this meal.

Afterwards, the servants set about clearing the great hall and kitchens. Meanwhile, the lord looked to recreational activities, such as hunting or playing chess.

The lady of the castle spent the day checking on the servants, making sure that the food supplies were plentiful and organizing accommodation for guests. This lady is having a rest and listening to some minstrels.

An evening meal was served late in the day – often just before bedtime. The lord and his family would then retire to their sleeping quarters while the workers cleared away the meal, prepared for the following day's tasks, and finally settled down to sleep.

Banquets and feasts

Eating was a very popular pastime in the castle. In medieval times, the wealthier you were, the better your diet. However, most people who lived and worked in a castle ate fairly well.

The staple foods of a castle-dweller's diet were bread, cheese and vegetables. Bees were often kept so that honey could be collected and used to sweeten food. The very best meats, such as venison, were only eaten by the lord and his highest officials. But even the servants, who ate much plainer food, were given meat occasionally.

At this **lavish** banquet in 1460, peacock is served as the main course.

Fish or fowl?

During the Middle Ages, the church **decreed** that no meat except fish could be eaten on certain days. To get around this, the barnacle goose was described as a fish so that lords and ladies were free to eat the meat at any time.

Meals provided not only essential food, but also the opportunity for entertainment. Lavish banquets demonstrated the lord's wealth and generosity and were used to impress guests and visitors. Exotic foods, such as peacock and swan, may have been served during a banquet. Food was sometimes even dyed to make it look more appealing.

Diners were often entertained by minstrels, acrobats and **jesters** during a feast.

TABLE PLAN

During a banquet, diners sat at long tables, with the lord and his family seated at a 'top table'. The more important you were, the closer you sat to the lord's table, and the sooner you were served. The further away you sat, the colder and plainer the food became.

Healthcare and hygiene were quite basic in medieval castles. However, people did what they could to keep clean and healthy.

Fresh water was supplied to the castle from a well. Some castles had a shaft in the wall so that water could be drawn up to different floors.

Castles had toilets called garderobes. The garderobe was simply a stone or wooden seat over a long shaft. The shaft emptied straight into the moat or into a pit called a cesspool. If the castle owner was wealthy, the garderobe might have had a washbasin, too.

This castle garderobe has a posh wooden seat. Many garderobes simply had a stone seat above the long waste shaft.

Feeling the chill

With the open shaft below, garderobes were extremely cold and draughty. The lord and his family used chamber pots instead. These were emptied into the moat by servants.

Baths were taken in tubs like barrels. The tub was moved to the warmest place possible – outside during the summer and by the fireside during the winter. Only a few castles had a bathroom, such as Leeds Castle in Kent.

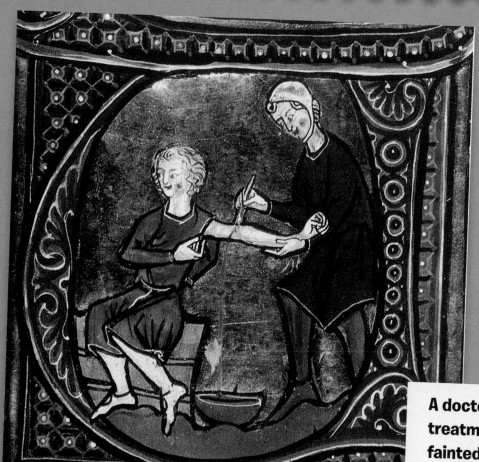

There was often a doctor who lived in the castle. The cure for many illnesses was bloodletting. The doctor cut a vein open and let blood drain out of it. The lord's wife was usually able to mix herbal medicines, too.

A doctor performs the medieval treatment of bloodletting. If a patient fainted during the process, they were thought to be on the road to recovery.

THE BLACK DEATH

All of the inhabitants of Cainhoe Castle, in Bedfordshire, England, died of the plague between 1348 and 1349. The 'black death', as it was known, was a terrible disease that killed millions of people across Europe during the 14th century.

Religion

Religion was very important in medieval times. Every castle had at least one chapel as well as a **chaplain**. The lord and lady attended chapel every day.

The chaplain was in charge of religious life in the castle. Chaplains could read and write, so they also wrote the castle **records** and helped to run the lord's **estate**. Sometimes chaplains gave lessons to children, too.

The chapel was often the highest room in a castle so that there was nothing between the chapel and heaven.

In times of need

Knights and soldiers may not necessarily have attended chapel every week. But when a battle was looming, you can be sure that they would have prayed to God to keep them safe.

Offering charity was considered necessary to be a good Christian. Many castles employed an almoner who took alms (money) and leftover food to the poor.

Castle workers were given the day off during most religious festivals, or holy days. Actors would act out scenes from the Bible to entertain the crowds. However, Christmas was a different matter. Lords and ladies liked to celebrate Christmas with lavish feasts, which had to be cooked and served by the castle staff.

Holy days were a time of celebration for all. Here, castle workers watch a visiting performer while enjoying a rare day off.

A FESTIVE APPETITE

In 1206, King John held a Christmas feast at Winchester Castle. His order included 1,500 chickens, 5,000 eggs, 20 oxen, 100 pigs and 100 sheep.

Entertainment

Though life in the castle was hard for the servants and workers, the lord and his family had lots more time for fun and games. Many types of entertainment took place in the castle.

Some lords hired a jester who would live in the castle and entertain the lord and his guests from sunrise to sunset. Other entertainers, such as mime artists, jugglers and acrobats, were paid to amuse diners during banquets. Storytellers and poets were often hired to give readings, too.

Jesters wore colourful outfits that made fun of fashionable clothes. They told jokes and sang funny (and sometimes rude) songs.

Musicians travelled around the country performing in castles and towns. They were paid, not only for their music, but also to carry news and gossip to and from the different places that they visited.

Games were played, such as **backgammon** and card games. Gambling with dice may also have been popular, especially with the castle's soldiers. However, the most exciting game was chess. Popular with knights as a game of war and **tactics**, it was also played by kings and nobles. Chess pieces were carefully carved out of wood or **ivory**.

King Otto IV of Brandenburg enjoys a game of chess with a lady.

CHESS DANGER

Playing chess could be a risky business. Bad losers might beat and even stab their winning rival. One man is said to have been battered with the chessboard after daring to beat the king!

Outdoor pursuits

As castles were cold and dingy, everyone preferred to spend time outside during the summer months. The nobles and peasants alike enjoyed a variety of outdoor pursuits.

Hunting was the most popular sport. As well as providing the thrill of the chase, it also put meat on the table and gave soldiers a chance to practise their shooting skills. The most popular weapon was usually a bow and arrow, though spears, swords and crossbows were also used.

Few women went hunting, but they often took part in falconry. No weapons were used in this sport. Instead, trained birds of prey flew from a noble's wrist to catch small animals and birds.

In this modern re-enactment, a lady releases a hawk as she demonstrates the sport of falconry. In medieval times, ladies rode **side-saddle** and were only allowed to hunt with female **merlins**.

Jousting tournaments provided another form of outdoor entertainment. Two knights rode towards each other on horseback, set on a dangerous collision course. The aim was to unseat your rival (knock him off his horse) using a long spear called a lance. Tournaments often featured wrestling, archery and sword fighting to entertain the crowds, too.

Jousting was a popular form of entertainment in the Middle Ages. Contestants often used blunted weapons in order to avoid seriously injuring each other.

Hand it over

Knights risked losing everything in a jousting tournament. Defeated knights often had to hand over both their horse and armour to the winner.

Children's lives

With all the hustle and bustle, castle life was probably fun for children. Childhood lasted until the age of seven, when training began.

Medieval children played with toys made of natural materials, such as wood and leather. Toys included dolls, balls, hobby horses, spinning tops, rattles, marbles, whistles and hoops. Puppets were also popular. Children played sports, too, including early forms of football and hockey.

Medieval children play an early form of football. A pig's bladder was used for a ball and there weren't really any rules.

At the age of seven, noble children were often sent to and from different castles to be trained by their relatives. Girls were sent away to learn how to be good wives. Boys began to train as pages. This meant that they might one day become knights.

Education was generally poor within the castle, unless you were lucky enough to be selected to train as a knight. The chaplain may have found time to teach some children to read and write. Peasant children sometimes got the opportunity to train as an apprentice in one of the trades, such as carpentry.

At around the age of 14, noble boys would continue their knight training as squires. They would begin to learn how to fight and use weapons.

Punishment

Criminals were punished severely during the Middle Ages. Most castles had a dungeon where people were imprisoned and tortured.

The penalty for serious crime was execution by hanging. The heads of **traitors** were cut off and displayed on the castle battlements, as a warning to others. For less serious crimes, there was a large variety of painful and embarrassing punishments.

The pillory This was a wooden frame with holes to grip the criminal's hands and head. Peasants would often throw rotten vegetables at the helpless individual, or, if the crime was serious, stones.

This modern re-enactment shows a young man trapped in the pillory. His captor taunts him by threatening to chop off his head.

Ducking In this punishment, the offender was strapped into a seat called the 'ducking stool' and lowered into the castle moat for short periods of time. Remember, there wasn't just water in the moat – the garderobes emptied into it, too!

Branding Some offences were punished by burning marks on to the criminal's body with a hot branding iron. This meant that they would be recognized as criminals throughout their lives. Offenders were often branded on the hand or face.

This illustration shows the punishment given to bakers who lied about the weight of their bread. The offender was dragged through the streets on a sled with bread tied around his neck.

BURNED TO THE GROUND

In 1088, Richard de Clare led a rebellion against the king. The rebellion was short-lived and de Clare was forced to surrender. His castle and the surrounding town of Tonbridge were burned as punishment.

Glossary

allot to assign or give

backgammon a board game where players throw dice to move their pieces around the board

butler a servant who kept the buttery and cellar well-stocked with drink

chaplain the person in charge of religious life in the castle

decree to give an official decision or order

estate a large area of land that is owned by one person

falconry a sport in which birds of prey are used to hunt small animals

feudal system the class structure of medieval society

forge to hammer and bend hot metal into shape

inhabitants all the people that live in a place

ivory the white substance in the tusks of animals such as elephants or hippos

jester a medieval performer who was paid to entertain by telling jokes and playing the fool

lavish extravagant and expensive

livestock farm animals

Mass a religious service in a church or chapel

medieval describes the period of the Middle Ages in Europe from the 5th to the 15th centuries

merlin a small falcon

Middle Ages the medieval period of history, between the 5th century and the 15th century

noble someone who has a high social rank, such as a lord, lady, duke or baron

pantler a servant who was in charge of stocking the pantry

peasants people who worked on a lord's land; the lowest class in the medieval feudal system

produce food that is grown

records a written account of life in the castle

side-saddle a way of sitting on a horse where both feet are on the same side

siege an attack by enemy forces in which a castle is cut off from supplies

tactics a plan to achieve success

tapestry a piece of heavy cloth woven with colourful scenes, often used as a wall hanging in castles

traitor a person who has betrayed his or her country

Further reading

Castle Diary by Richard Platt (Walker, 2011)

Castles by Stephanie Turnbull (Usborne, 2006)

Castles (Medieval World) by Sean Sheehan (Franklin Watts, 2006)

Did Castles Have Bathrooms? by Ann Kerns (Lerner, 2010)

Everything Castles by Crispin Boyer (National Geographic Kids, 2011)

The World's Most Amazing Castles by Ann Weil (Raintree, 2011)

What Were Castles For? by Phil Roxbee Cox (Usborne, 2002)

Websites

http://www.castles.me.uk/medieval-castles.htm
Explore medieval life in a castle on this informative website.

http://www.castles.org/Kids_Section/Castle_Story
Find out what goes on inside a castle on this interesting website.

http://www.kidsonthenet.com/castle/view.html
Explore this castle to find out about everything from hawks to tournaments.

http://www.pictures-of-castles.co.uk
Find hundreds of pictures of different castles around Britain.

Index

SERIES CONTENTS

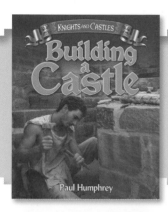

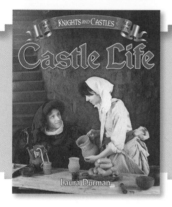
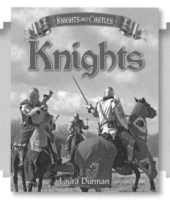